A Fine and Private Place

Here lyes
HENRY PVRCELL Esqr
Who left this Life
And is gone to that Blessed Place
Where only his Harmony
can be exceeded
Obijt 21mo die Novembrs
Anno Ætatis suæ 37mo
Annoq. Domini 1695

A FINE AND PRIVATE PLACE

A collection of Epitaphs and Inscriptions
chosen by

Joan Bakewell & John Drummond

with photographs by
Andrew Lawson

Weidenfeld & Nicolson
London

Weidenfeld and Nicolson
11 St John's Hill, London SW11

Designed by Tim Higgins

ISBN 0 297 77432 8

Filmset in Monophoto *Spectrum*
by Keyspools Ltd, Golborne, Lancs
Printed in Great Britain by
Morrison & Gibb Ltd, London and Edinburgh

ACKNOWLEDGMENTS

It is a pleasure to join the long list of authors who are
in the debt of the London Library. We would also like
to acknowledge the contribution and advice of
numerous incumbents of British churches and of many
friends including Lady Diana Cooper, Alec Clifton Taylor,
Richard Demarco, the Rev. E. A. J. Emery,
Jack Emery, Alan Glencross and Martin Kinna.

INTRODUCTION

THIS IS A PERSONAL BOOK. It has its origins in a shared love of British country churchyards, and a regret that many of their tombstones are falling into decay. We also find in the recorded grief of earlier generations some redress for today's failure to come to terms with death.

There have been previous collections of British epitaphs: few are readily accessible today. Their intentions have for the most part been exhaustively antiquarian or wryly humorous. Many have included epitaphs written simply as a literary form and never intended for transfer to stone. Some concentrate on the famous, and neglect the modest statement. Many also perpetuate arch, jokey or punning epitaphs that might have served – but often turn out to be spurious. This book does none of these things.

Our selection of words and pictures has been chosen primarily for aesthetic reasons. In considering literally thousands of epitaphs, we have preferred always an unexpected or surprising beauty of language, expression or appearance. We have not excluded the acrostic, the anagram, or the joke; we have simply included our favourites. As far as we have been able to ascertain all of them do or did once exist as memorials on wood, stone or brass to the people they commemorate. But we have allowed one or two borderline cases to remain. Where possible we include date and place: but this is not a field guide. The original spelling has been retained, except where intelligibility has required its updating. County boundaries are similarly revised. We hope in this way to preserve what is attractive from the past while making it accessible today.

The pictures complement the text sometimes by showing the setting of a quoted epitaph, more usually by conveying the strange and moving beauty of different ways of marking death. Always we seek to share our pleasure in a form that is itself dying. It has proved impossible to discover recent examples of epitaphs that bear comparison with the best of the past. Not only is death a taboo subject in our society; the epitaph – death's record – is no longer something to which we give serious thought. For this reason alone it would seem worth while looking back – in these pages – to the best that has been.

J.B. J.D. A.L.

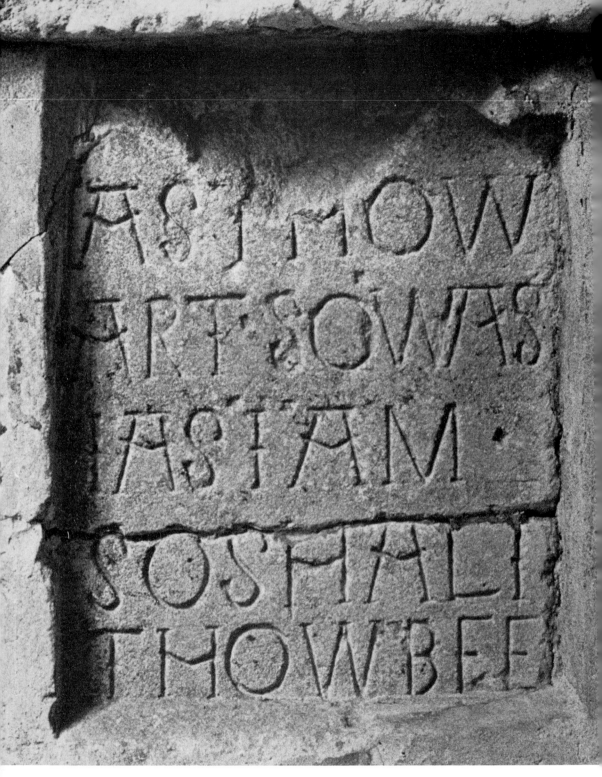

St Eadburgha's, Broadway,
Hereford and Worcester

AS THOW
ART SO WAS
I. AS I AM
SO SHALT
THOW BEE.

Shall we all die
We shall die all
All die shall we
Die all we shall

Gunwalloe, Cornwall

Ann Marsden, died 1811, aged 30

Here lies the breathless sight,
Which lately was my comfort and delight ;
Just on the verge of joy my hopes are fled
The offspring lives but oh ! the mother's dead.

Bakewell, Derbyshire

Jane Parker, died 1653

Heare lyeth a midwife brought to bed,
Deliveresse Delivered ;
Her body being Churched here
Her soule gives thanks in yonder sphere.

Peterborough Cathedral,
Cambridgeshire

Edward Seymour, infant son of
William Seymour, Earl of Hertford, died 1631

Speechless tho' yet he were, say all we can
That saw, he promise did a hopefull man.
Such frame of body, such a holy soule,
Argu'd him written in the long liv'd roule.
But now wee see, by such an infant's losse,
All are but infant hopes, which death may crosse.

Collingbourne Ducis, Wiltshire

John Holbin, died 1812, aged 9

I cried O Lord spare my child.
He did, but not as I meant.
He snatched it from danger
and took it to his own home.

By accident my life was spent
It was what the Lord thought fit.
My parents dear your grief forbear
To Death we must submit.

Kelston, Avon

William and John May, brothers, died 1661

Two brethren much endear'd, who us'd to have
In Life one Heart and Purse, have now one grave.

St Margaret's, King's Lynn, Norfolk

Mrs Sarah Mills and
Mrs Rebecca Ward

Under this stone, in easy slumber lies
Two dusty bodies, that at last shall rise:
Their parted atoms shall again rejoin,
Be cast into new moulds by hands divine.

Crostwick, Norfolk

The Hon. Robert Digby
and his Sister Mary, erected by their
Father the Lord Digby, Anno 1729

Go! fair Example of untainted Youth,
Of modest Wisdom, and pacific Truth;
Compos'd in Sufferings, and in Joy Sedate,
Good without Noise, without Pretension great:
Just of thy Word, in ev'ry Thought sincere,
Who knew no Wish, but what the World might hear:
Of softest Manners, unaffected Mind,
Lover of Peace, and Friend of human Kind:
Go live! for Heaven's eternal Year is thine;
Go, and exalt thy mortal to Divine.

And thou, blest Maid, Attendant on his Doom,
Pensive hast follow'd to the silent Tomb,
Steer'd the same Course to the same quiet Shore,
Not parted long, and now to part no more!
Go then, where only Bliss sincere is known!
Go, where to love and to enjoy are one!

Yet take these Tears, Mortality's Relief,
And till we share your Joys, forgive our Grief:
These little Rites, a Stone, a Verse, receive,
'Tis all a Father, all a Friend, can give.

Written by ALEXANDER POPE,
Sherborne Abbey, Dorset

Mrs Pritchard, actress, died 1761, aged 57

Her Comic Vein had every Charm to please,
'Twas Nature's Dictates breath'd with Nature's Ease.
Ev'n when her Powers sustain'd the Tragic Load,
Full, clear, and just, th' harmonious Accents flow'd;
And the big Passions of her feeling Heart
Burst freely forth, and sham'd the Mimic Art.

Oft on the Scene, with Colours not her own
She painted Vice, and taught us what to shun.
One virtuous Track her real Life pursu'd
That nobler Part was uniformly good;
Each Duty there to such Perfection wrought,
That if the Precepts fail'd, the Example taught.

Westminster Abbey, London

Thomas Jackson, actor, died 1798, aged 56

Thomas Jackson, Comedian,
who was engaged 21st of Dec. 1741, to play a
comic cast of characters, in this great theatre
the World; for many of which he was
prompted by nature to excel.

The season being ended, his benefit over,
the charges all paid, and his account closed,
he made his exit in the tragedy of Death, on
the 17th of March, 1798, in full assurance of
being called once more to rehearsal, where
he hopes to find his forfeits all cleared, his
cast of parts bettered, and his situation made
agreeable, by him who paid the great stock-
debt, for the love he bore to performers
in general.

Gillingham, Norfolk

John the Smith, died 1370

Man com & se how schal alle dede be; wen yow comes bad & bare;
Noth hav ben be alway fare: all ys werines yt be for care:
Bot yt be do for godys luf we have nothyng yare. Hundyr
Yis grave lys John ye smyth. God zif hys soule heven grit.

Brightwell Baldwin, Oxfordshire

John Smith, Governor of Virginia, died 1631

Here lies one conquer'd that hath conquer'd Kings,
Subdu'd large Territories, and done Things
Which to the World impossible would seem,
But that the Truth is held in more Esteem.
Shall I report his former Service done
In Honour of his God and Christendom?
How that he did divide from Pagans three,
Their Heads and Lives, Types of his Chivalry?
For which great Service in that Climate done,
Brave Sigismundus, King of Hungarion,
Did give him as a Coat of Arms to wear,
These conquer'd Heads, got by his Sword and Spear.
Or shall I tell of his Adventures since
Done in Virginia, that large Continent?
How that he subdu'd Kings unto his Yoke,
And made those Heathens flee as Wind does Smoke:
And made their Land, being of so large a Station,
An Habitation for our Christian Nation;
Where God is glorified, their Wants supply'd
Which else for Necessaries must have dy'd?

But what avails his Conquest, now he lies
Interr'd in Earth, a Prey to Worms and Flies?
O! may his Soul in sweet Elysium sleep,
Untill the Keeper that all Souls doth keep,
Return to Judgment; and that after thence,
With Angels he may have his Recompence.

St Sepulchre's, Holborn, London

James Barker, died 1749

Reader,
If fond of what is rare, attend!
Here lies an honest man,
Of perfect Piety,
Of Lamblike Patience,
My friend James Barker;
to whom I pay this mean
Memorial for what deserves the greatest.
An example
which shone thro' all
the Clouds of Fortune,
illustrious in low Estate,
the Lesson and Reproach of those above him.
To lay this little Stone
is my Ambition;
While others rear
the Pompous Marbles of the great.
Vain Pomp!
a Turf o'er Virtue charms us more.

Written by EDWARD YOUNG
Welwyn, Hertfordshire

Death is a fisherman; the world we see
A fish pond is, and we the fishes be;
He sometimes angles, like doth with us play,
And slily takes us one by one away.

High Wycombe, Buckinghamshire

Ann Handen, died 1816, aged 53

Time rolls his ceaseless course; the race of yore
Who danced our infancy upon their knees,
And told our marvelling childhood legends store
Of their strange ventures, happ'd by sea or land,
How are they blotted from the things that be;
How few, all weak and wither'd of the force,
Wait on the verge of dark eternity,
Like stranded wrecks, – the tide returning hoarse,
To snatch them from our sight – Time rolls his
      ceaseless course.

Hastings, Sussex

Long Melford, Suffolk

In Christian Hope
Of a BLESSED IMORTALITY
Near This Place Lyeth Inter'd
The Body of IANE, late Wife
Of MATTHEW HVMBERSTONE
Of London Esq.ʳ The Second Daughter
Of Iames Hoste of Sandringam in Nor=
=folk Esq.ʳ Who Being a Person of Singular
Accomplishm.ᵗˢ And Many Excellent Vertues
Her Endeared Husband Thinks This Monum.ᵗ
Amost Iust Debt To Her Fragrant Memory,
She Dy'd Iuly y.ᵉ J7.ᵗʰ J694.
In Her 33.ʳᵈ year.

Her noble Soul and lovely body joyn'd
Were once the joy and wonder of mankind.
They who have known her thus, with sighs confess
They wish they'd known her still, or known her less
Her Race was short, the longer is her Rest
God Onely wise disposes all things best.

Her Husband
MATTHEW HVMBERSTONE
also Departed this life y.ᵉ
28.ᵗʰ day of August 1709
Aged 60 years

Nil non Mortale tenemus

If Bloud or Beauty Parts or Grace could Save
from the Corruptions of the Comōn Grave
or Without Death conferre Divinitie
we might have wondred this Deare S^T. did dye
But since to Bliss Death must Induction give
of Need Shee dy'd that Shee might better live
dy'd, Ah too Early! yet let none Complaine
This was Necessity, That was her Gaine.

Above Fulbrook, Oxfordshire
Opposite St Olave's, Hart Street, City of London
Below Edwardstone, Suffolk

MEMORIÆ SACRVM.
TO Y PRECIOVS MEMORY OF
BENIAMIN BRAND, OF EDWARDSTONE HAL, ESQ; AND
ELIZABETH HIS WIFE;
WHOM, WHEN PROVIDENCE, AFTER 35 YEARES CONIVNCTION, DIVIDED;
DEATH, AFTER 12 DAYES DIVORCEM, REVNITED:
WHO, LEAVEING THEIR RARE EXAMPLES
TO 6 SONNES AND 6 DAVGHTERS,
(ALL NVRSD WITH HER VNBORROWED MILK)
BLEST WITH POOREMENS PRAYRES: EMBAVLMD W^TH NVMEROVS TEARES;
LYE, HERE, REPOSED.

Sir Charles Cavendish, died 1617

Sonnes seeke not me among those polish'd stones,
These only hide part of my flesh and bones,
Which did they ne're so neate, or proudly dwell,
Will all be dust, and may not make me swell.

Let such as justly have out-liv'd all prayse,
Trust in the Tombes their carefull Frends do raise,
I made my life my Monument, and yours,
To which there's no Materiall that endures.

Nor yet Inscription like it. Write but that,
And teach your Nephews it to aemulate.
It will be matter loude inough to tell
Not when I died, but how I liv'd. Farewell.

Bolsover, Derbyshire

Above The Farnham tomb, Quorndon, Leicestershire
Below Tomb of Thomas Bromley, Westminster Abbey

Mrs Ann Cowper, died 1737,
by her son, William Cowper

HERE *lies interr'd, too soon bereft of life,*
The best of mothers, and the kindest wife:
Who neither knew, nor practis'd any art,
Secure in all she wish'd, her husband's heart;
Her love to him preserving ev'n in death,
Pray'd heav'n to bless him with her latest breath.
Still was she studious never to offend,
And glad of an occasion to commend:
With ease could pardon injuries receiv'd,
Nor e'er was cheerful when another griev'd:
Despising state, with her own lot content,
Enjoy'd the comforts of a life well-spent;
Resign'd when Heav'n demanded back her breath,
Her mind heroic 'midst the pangs of death.
Whoe'er thou art that dost this tomb draw near,
O stay a while, and shed a friendly tear;
These lines, tho' weak, are like herself sincere.

Berkhamsted, Hertfordshire

The Rev. William Edwards,
by his son, the Rev. Robert Edwards

The Ritual Stone thy Son doth lay
  O'er thy respected Dust,
Only proclaims the mournful Day
  When he a Parent lost.
Fame will convey thy Virtues down
  Thro' Ages yet to come;
'Tis needless, since so well they're known,
  To crowd them on thy Tomb.
Deep to engrave them on my Heart,
  Rather demands my Care:
Oh! cou'd I stamp in ev'ry Part
  The fair Impression there!
In Life to copy thee I'll strive,
  And, when I that resign,
May some good-natur'd Friend survive,
  To lay my Bones by thine!

Cleobury Mortimer, Shropshire

Mary, Lady Digby, died 1692

Whom it were unpardonable to lay down in silence,
And of whom 'tis difficult to speak with justice.
For her just character will look like Flattery
And the least abatement of this injury to her Memory
In every condition of Life She was a pattern to her Sex
Appear'd Mistress of those peculiar qualities
That were requisite to conduct her through it with Honour
And never fail'd to exert them in their proper Seasons
With the utmost advantage.
She was modest without Affectation
Easy without Levity and reserved without Pride
Knew how to stoop without Sinking
And to gain Peoples Affections without lessening their regards.
She was carefull without Anxiety,
Frugal without Parsimony,
Not at all fond of the superfluous trappings of Greatness.
Yet abridged herself in nothing that her Quality required.
She was a faithfull Member of the Church of England.
Her Piety was exemplary, her Charity universal,
She found herself a Widow in the beginning of her Life
When the temptations of Beauty, Honour, Youth, and Pleasure
Were in their full Strength,
Yet she made them all give way to the interest of her Family,
And betook herself entirely to the Matron's part:
The Education of her Children engross'd all her Cares,
No charge was spared in the cultivation of their minds
Nor any pains in the improvement of their Fortunes,

In a Word,
She was truly Wise, truly Honourable, and truly Good,
More can scarce be said,
And yet he that says this, knew her well
And is well assured he has said nothing
Which either Veracity or Modesty should oblige him to
suppress.

Coleshill, Warwickshire

Jean Anderson, died 1770

Praises on Tombs are vainly spent:
A good Name is a Monument.

Hammersmith, London

Robert Lowe, died 1853, aged 37

In the prime of life
And the vigour of his days
He was suddenly called from
A close connection with the
Church Militant to join
The Church Triumphant.

Bakewell, Derbyshire

James Pickering, died 1757, aged 59

A Soul prepar'd needs no Delay ;
The Summons comes, the Saints obey.
Swift was his Flight, and short the Road ;
He clos'd his Eyes, and saw his God.
The Flesh lies here till Jesus come
To claim the Treasure from the Tomb.

Waltham Abbey, Essex

Nathaniel Burnell, killed by
a threshing machine 1856, aged 7

He was suddenly summoned hence but his
lamp was trimmed and his light burning.

Withycombe, Somerset

Unknown, dated 1727

With sighs and tears grieve not your heart
  Nor think my fate is hard
There's no such thing as sudden death
  To those that are prepared.

Ston Easton, Somerset

The Rev. John Rudd,
died 1640, aged 72

Son of Thunder, Son of the Dove,
Full of hot zeal, full of trewe love.
In preaching Truth, in living right,
A burning Lamp, a shining Light.

Sheepsdale, Berwickshire

William Salter

Here lies Will Salter, honest man,
Deny it, Envy, if you can:
True to his business and his trust,
Always punctual, always just;
His horses, could they speak, would tell,
They loved their good old master well.
His up-hill work is chiefly done,
His stage is ended, race is run;
One journey is remaining still,
To climb up Sion's holy hill.
And now his faults are all forgiven,
Elijah like, drives up to heaven,
Takes the reward of all his pains,
And leaves to other hands the reins.

Haddiscoe, Norfolk

Robert Gilbert, died 1714

In wise Frugality luxuriant,
In Justice & Good Actes extravagant,
To all the world an universal Friend,
No foe to any but the savage kind.
How many fair estates have been grac'd
By the same generous means; yet his increas'd.
His duty thus perform'd to Heaven & Earth,
Each leisure hour fresh toilsome sports gave birth.
Had NIMROD *seen, he would ye game decline,*
To GILBERT *mighty hunter's name resign:*
Tho' hundreds to the grounds he oft has chas'd,
That subtle Fox Death earth'd him here at last,
And left a fragrant scent so sweet behind
That ought to be pursu'd by all mankind.

Cantley, Norfolk

Robert Graye, died 1635, aged 65

Consecrated To The Blessed Memory Of
Robert Graye Esq. And Founder.

Taunton Bore Him : London Bred Him:
Piety Train'd Him : Virtue Led Him:
Earth Enrich'd Him : Heaven Carest Him:
Taunton Blest Him : London Blest Him:
This Thankful Town : That Mindful City:
Share His Piety And His Pity.
What He Gave, And How He Gave It,
Ask The Poor And You Shall Have It.

Gentle Reader, Heaven May Strike
Thy Tender Heart To Do The Like.
Now Thine Eyes Have Read The Story,
Give Him The Praise, And GOD *The Glory.*

Taunton, Somerset

Bury St Edmunds Cathedral, Suffolk

Sarah y^e Wife of Ed.
Worton dyed y^e 7 of
Nou. :1698: Aged 69
Good people all as you
Pas by, looke round
See how Corpes do lye
For as you are som time Ware We
and as we are so must you be

IN MEMORY OF
Mr IOHN MATTINSON
BORN IN LONG SLEDDALE
NEAR KENDALE WESTMORE
=LAND, HE WAS ELEVEN
YEARS THE BELOVED
SCHOOL MASTER OF THIS
TOWN, AND THEN UNFOR=
=TUNATELY SHOT, THE 23
OF NOVEM.ber 1723 AGED 32

Here lies Interred the Body of
MARY HASELTON
A Young Maiden of this Town,
Born of Roman Catholic Parents
And Virtuously brought up.
Who being in the Act of Prayer
Repeating Her Vespers.
Was instantaneously killed by a flash
Of lightning August the 16th 1785,
Aged 9 Years.

Above East Bergholt, Suffolk
Below Bury St Edmunds Cathedral, Suffolk

Opposite Kensal Green Cemetery, London

Sir Francis Vere, died 1609

When VERE *fought Death, arm'd with his Sword and Shield,*
Death was afraid to meet him in the Field:
But when his Weapons he had laid aside,
Death like a Coward strook him, and he dy'd.

Westminster Abbey, London

Tomb of Sir Francis Vere, Westminster Abbey

George Routleigh, died 1802, aged 57

Here lies, in horizontal position,
the outside case of
GEORGE ROUTLEIGH, watchmaker;
Whose abilities in that line were an honour
to his profession.
Integrity was the Mainspring, and prudence the
Regulator,
of all the actions of his life.
Humane, generous, and liberal,
his Hand never stopped
till he had relieved distress.
So nicely regulated were all his motions,
that he never went wrong,
except when set a-going
by people
who did not know his Key:
even then he was easily
set right again.
He had the art of disposing his time so well
that his hours glided away
in one continual round
of pleasure and delight,
till an unlucky minute put a period to
his existence.
He departed this life
Nov. 14, 1802,
aged 57:
wound up,
in hopes of being taken in hand
by his Maker;
and of being thoroughly cleaned, repaired,
and set a-going
in the world to come.

Lydford, Devon

In memory of JOHN STONE
Parish Clerk 41 years
Excellent in his way
Buried here 26 May 1727
Aged 78.

Holy Trinity, Hull,
Humberside

Thomas Whitebred, died 1684, aged 99

Softly, Friend, softly, check thy saucy foot,
That rudely tramples near this aged dust,
That dust, whilst into life and vigour put,
Made the third sister her own act mistrust;
The fatal knife a..nost a century
Rusty and blunt and useless laid by:
Till in her fearful hand the blade she took,
And shook, and trembled when she gave the stroake.
When others left off living he began,
A youth at fourty, and at sixty man;
His strength and parts at seventy in their prime,
Other's October was but May with him.
Undauntedly he fought for two good Kings,
Princes as great as were their sufferings.
Till prest with years the fatal union broake,
And then down, ah! down fell this sturdy oake.
The fatning Dew which on the Branches fell,
*   Cheard and supply'd the wants of all below.*

Great Baddow, Essex

John Savage, aged 24

Here, Reader, mark, perhaps now in thy Prime,
The stealing Steps of never-standing Time:
Thou'lt be what I am! Catch the present Hour;
Employ that well, for that's within thy Pow'r.

Croydon, Surrey

Anne Burton, died 1642, aged 15

Reader, stand back; dull not this Marble Shrine,
With irreligious Breath: the Stone's divine,
And does enclose a Wonder Beauty, Wit,
Devotion, and Virginity with it.
Which, like a Lilly fainting in its Prime,
Wither'd and left the World; deceitful Time
Crop it too soon: And Earth, the self-same Womb
From whence it sprung, is now become the Tomb.
Whose sweeter Soul, a Flower of matchless Price,
Transplanted is from hence to Paradise.

Oakham, Leicestershire

Sixteen years a maiden,
One twelve Month's a wife,
One half hour a mother,
And then I Lost my life.

Folkestone, Kent

She took the cup of life to sip,
Too bitter't was to drain;
She put it meekly from her lip,
And went to sleep again.

All Saints, Cambridge

How vain a thing is man,
When God thinks meet
Oftimes with swaddling clothes
To join the winding sheet.
A web of forty weeks
Spun forth in pain,
To his dear parents' grief,
Soon ravelled out again,
This babe, intombed
Upon the world did peep,
Disliked it, clos'd its eyes,
Fell fast asleep.

St Michael-le-Belfrey, York

The Hon. Alexina Duncan, died 1824, aged 16

Bring flowers, pale flowers, o'er the grave to shed
A crown for the brow of the early dead
Though they smile in vain for what once was ours
They are love's last gift, bring ye flowers, pale flowers.

Written by Mrs Hemans,
Bathampton, Avon

Near this place lie the bodies of
JOHN HEWET and MARY DREW,
an industrious young Man
and virtuous Maiden of this Parish;
Who, being at Harvest Work
(with several others)
were in one instant killed by Lightning
the last day of July 1718.

Think not, by rig'rous Judgment seiz'd
A Pair so faithful could expire;
Victims so pure Heav'n saw well pleas'd,
And snatch'd them in celestial fire.

Live well, and fear no sudden fate;
When God calls Virtue to the grave,
Alike 'tis Justice soon or late,
Mercy alike to kill or save.

Virtue unmov'd can hear the call,
And face the flash that melts the ball.

Stanton Harcourt, Oxfordshire

John Abdidge, Alderman,
died 1785

Of no distemper,
Of no blast he died,
But fell,
Like Autumn's fruit,
That mellows long,
Even wondered at
Because he dropt not sooner.
Providence seemed to wind him up
For fourscore years
Yet ran he nine winters more;
Till, like a clock,
Worn out with repeating time,
The wheels of weary life
At last stood still.

High Wycombe,
Buckinghamshire

William Lawrence, died 1621, aged 29

With diligence and trust most exemplary
Did William Lawrence serve a prebendary,
And for his pains now past before not lost
Gained this remembrance at his masters cost.

O read these lines again : you seldom find
A servant faithful and a master kind.

Short hand he wrote, his flower in prime did fade
And hasty death short hand of him hath made.
Well couth he numbers and well measured land,
Thus doth he now that ground whereon you stand
Wherein he lyes so geometrical :
Art maketh some but thus will nature all.

Westminster Abbey, London

Marya Arundell, died 1629

MARYA ARUNDELL: MAN A DRY LAURELL

Man to the marigold compar'd may bee,
Men may be liken'd to the laurell tree :
Both feede the eye – both please the optic sense ;
Both soone decaye – both suddenly fleete hence ;
What then infer you from her name but this
Man fades away – Man a dry Laurell is.

Duloe, Cornwall

Dorothy Selby, needlewoman, who
traditionally disclosed the Gunpowder Plot

She was a Dorcas
Whose curious needle wound the abused stage
Of this lewd world into the golden age,
Whose pen of steel and silken ink enrolled
The acts of Jonah in records of gold.
Whose art disclosed that plot, which, had it taken,
Rome had triumphed and Britain's walls been shaken.

She was
In heart a Lydia, and in tongue a Hannah,
In zeal a Ruth, in wedlock a Susanna
Prudently simple, providently wary,
To the world a Martha, and to Heaven a Mary.

Who put on ⎫ in the year of ⎧ Pilgrimage 69
immortality ⎭   her   ⎨ Redeemer 1641

Ightham, Kent

Monument to Dorothy Selby

To the pretious name and honor

Dame Dorothy Selby

Daughter and Heire

Whose ...... the abused Stage
Of the ...... golden Age
Whose Po ...... d the black enroll'd
The Arte o ...... rd of Gold
Whose Arte dis ...... rt which had it taken
Rome had ...... alls had shaken

In hear ...... uous Hanna
In Z ...... Susanna
Prude ...... Mary
To th' Worl ......

IMMORT

Above Bunhill Fields, London

Opposite, above The American cemetery, Brookwood, Surrey
Opposite, below Kensal Green Cemetery, London

Penelope Boothby,
died 1791, aged 9

She was in form and intellect
    Most exquisite
The unfortunate parents ventured
    Their all on this frail bark
And the wreck was total.

Ashbourne, Derbyshire

Tomb of Penelope Boothby, by Thomas Banks RA

Anthony Bond, died 1576

Christ is to me as life on earth, and death to me is gaine
Because I truste thorowe him alone salvation to obteyne :
So bryttle is the state of man, so soone it dothe decay,
So all the glory of ye worlde must passe and fade awaye.

Egham, Surrey

John Stevens, died 1811, aged 77

Slave to no sect, he took no private road,
But look'd through nature up to nature's God.

Hackney, London

William Marlphant, died 1806, aged 17

Believe, and look with triumph on the tomb!

Bermondsey, London

George Warren, died 1755

Keep Death and Judgment always in your Eye;
None are fit to live, who are not fit to die:
Make use of present Time, because you must
Take up your Lodging shortly in the Dust.
'Tis dreadful to behold the setting Sun,
And Night approaching, ere your Work is done.

Kew, Surrey

Joseph Crossman, died 1844, aged 25

In an instant I sank, neath the shadows of death,
*   And eternity round me arose!*
O! reader remember that life is a breath,
*   And a breath may bring thine to a close.*

Weare, Somerset

John Thatcher,
died 1622, aged 6

Under that stone's a chi
ld wrapt in earth's mold,
For whom canot his par
ents griefe be told.
In wit most rare noe
lesse in Grace was he ;
The sooner fit with
Christ in blis to be.

Milton Clevedon,
Somerset

John Chester, died 1640, aged 3

Griev'd at the world and crimes, this early bloome
Look'd round, and sigh'd, and stole into his tombe,
His fall was like his birth, too quick this rose
Made haste to spread, and the same haste to close.
Here lies his dust, but his best tomb's fled hence,
For marble cannot last like innocence.

Chicheley, Oxfordshire

Never was Innocence & Prudence
Soe lovely, that had you known
her conversation, you would have
said, she was the daughter of Eve
before she eated of the Apple.
She hath left her name
CATHERINE PARMINTER.
A.D. 1660

Ilfracombe, Devon

Mary Blackford, died 1669, aged 11

Short was her life, Long was her payne
Great was our loss, Much more her gayne.

Dunster, Somerset

Elizabeth Oldfield, died 1642

Here is the wardrobe of my dusty clothes
Which hands divine shall brush, and make so gay
That my immortal soul shall put them on
And wear the same upon my Wedding day.
In which attire my Lord shall me convoy
Then to the lodging of eternal joy.

Chipping Sodbury, Gloucestershire

As those we love decay, we die in part,
String after string is sever'd from the heart;
Till loosen'd life, at last but breathing clay,
Without one pang is glad to flee away;
Unhappy he! who latest feels the blow,
Whose eyes have wept o'er every friend laid low,
Dragg'd lingering on from partial death to death,
Till dying, all he can resign is breath.

Islington, London

Mary Sperring, died 1811, aged 42

While pale disease upon her vitals prey'd
Her strength exhausted and her frame decay'd
With painful steps life lingered to the grave
When human skill had lost the power to save
Yet still kind heaven disposed her virtuous mind
To live in patience & to die resign'd.

Radstock, Somerset

John Parsley, died 1828, aged 29

Condemn'd like me to hear the faint reply,
To mark the fading cheek and sinking eye,
From the chill brow to wipe the sweat of death,
And watch in dumb despair the parting breath,
If chance conducts you to this humble shrine,
Know gentle passenger these pangs were mine,
Ordain'd to lose the partner of my breast,
Whose kind affections charm'd and virtues blest,
Form'd every tie that binds the Heart to prove
His duty friendship and that friendship love,
The rising tear I check and kiss the rod,
And not to death resign him but to God.

Twerton, Avon

Thomas Turar, died 1643

Like to a Baker's Oven is the grave
Wherein the bodyes of the faithful have
A Setting in, and where they do remain
In hopes to Rise, and to be Drawn again;
Blessed are they who in the LORD are dead,
Though Set like Dough, they shall be Drawn like Bread.

All Saints, Bristol, Avon

In memory of JOHN TAYLOR, of Silkstone, potter, who
departed this life, July 14th, Anno Domini 1815, aged 72 years.
Also HANNAH, his wife, who departed this life,
August 13th, 1815, aged 68 years.

Out of the clay they got their daily bread,
Of clay were also made.
Returned to clay they now lie dead,
Where all that's left must shortly go.
To live without him his wife she tried,
Found the task hard, fell sick, and died.
And now in peace their bodies lay,
Until the dead be called away,
And moulded into spiritual clay.

Silkstone, South Yorkshire

Abraham Baby, died 1706

BENEATH THIS PLACE IN 6 FOOT IN LENGTH AGAINST YE
CLARK'S PEW LYETH THE BODY OF
MR. ABM. BABY,
ALSO YE BODY OF MARY HIS WID.
She dyed ye 21st May, 1705.
Also 2 Children of ye said Abm. and Mary, which dyed in
their enfantry.

Man's life is like untoe a winter's daye,
Some brake their faste, and so depart awaye.
Others stay dinner – then depart full fed.
The longest age but supps and goes to bed.
O reader, then behold and see
As we are now so must ye be.

Croyland, Lincolnshire

William Keeling, of the East India Company,
died 1619, aged 42

Fortie & two yeares in this Vessell fraile
On the rough Seas of Life did Keeling saile
A Merchant fortunate, a Captaine bould.
A Courtier gracious, yett alas! not old.
Such Worth, Experience, Honour & high Praise
Few winne in twice soe many yeares a daies.
But what ye worlde admired, he dem'd but drosse
For CHRIST; without Christ all his Gain but losse;
For Him & His deare Love, with merrie cheere
To the Holy Land his last course hee did steere:
Faith served for Sailes, the sacred Word for Cord,
Hope was his Anchor, Glorie his Reward:
And thus with gales of Grace, by happie Venter
Through Straits of Death, Heaven's Harbour he did enter.

Carisbrooke, Isle of Wight

William Braithwaite, smith, died 1757

My sledge and hammers lie reclin'd,
My bellows, too, have lost their wind,
My fire's extinct, my forge decay'd,
And in the dust my vice is lay'd.
My coal is spent, my fuel's gone,
My nails are drove, my work is done;
My fire-dry'd corpse lies here at rest,
My soul smoke-like's ascending to be blest.

St Alban's, Hertfordshire

In Memory Of
WILLIAM PICKERING,
who died Decr 24, 1845
AGED 30 YEARS

ALSO RICHARD EDGER
who died Decr 24, 1845
AGED 24 YEARS

THE SPIRITUAL RAILWAY
The Line to heaven by Christ was made
With heavenly truth the Rails are laid,
From Earth to Heaven the Line extends,
To Life Eternal where it ends
Repentance is the Station then
Where Passengers are taken in,
No Fee for them is there to pay
For Jesus is himself the way
God's Word is the first Engineer
It points the way to Heaven so dear,
Through tunnels dark and dreary here
It does the way to Glory steer.
God's Love the Fire, his Truth the Steam,
Which drives the Engine and the Train,
All you who would to Glory ride,
Must come to Christ, in him abide
In First and Second, and Third Class,
Repentance, Faith and Holiness,
You must the way to Glory gain
Or you with Christ will not remain
Come then poor Sinners, now's the time
At any Station on the Line
If you'll repent and turn from sin
The Train will stop and take you in.

Ely Cathedral, Cambridgeshire

SACRED
TO THE MEMORY OF THOMAS SCAIFE.

late an Engineer on the Birmingham and Gloucester Railway:
who lost his life at Bromsgrove Station by the Explosion of
an Engine Boiler   Tuesday the 10 of November 1840.

He was 28 Years of Age, highly esteemed by his fellow workmen
for his many amiable qualities, and his Death will be long lamentd
by all those who had the pleasure of his acquaintance.

The following lines were composed by an unknown Friend
as a Memento of the worthiness of the Deceased.

My *engine* now is cold and still   My *flanges* all refuse to guide.
No water does my *boiler* fill: My *clacks* also, though once so strong
My *coke* affords its flame no more.   Refuse to aid the busy throng
My days of usefulness are o'er   No more I feel each urging breath
My *wheels* deny their noted speed   My *steam* is now condens'd in death.
No more my guiding hands they heed   Life's *railway's* oe'r, each *station's* past.
My *whistle* too, has lost its tone   In death I'm stopp'd and rest at last.
Its shrill and thrilling sounds are gone   Farewell dear friends and cease to weep
My *valves* are now thrown open wide   In Christ I'm SAFE, in Him I sleep.

THIS STONE WAS ERECTED AT THE JOINT EXPENCE
OF HIS FELLOW WORKMEN 1842

PRATT EnGR

Bromsgrove, Hereford and Worcester

Above The Manners tomb, Bakewell, Derbyshire

Opposite Lewknor, Oxfordshire

IT IS THE FATE OF MOST MEN
TO HAVE MANY ENEMIES, AND FEW FRIENDS.
THIS MONUMENTAL PILE
IS NOT INTENDED TO MARK THE CAREER.
BUT TO SHEW
HOW MUCH ITS INHABITANT WAS RESPECTED
BY THOSE WHO KNEW HIS WORTH.
AND THE BENEFITS
DERIVED FROM HIS REMEDIAL DISCOVERY.
HE IS NOW AT REST
AND FAR BEYOND THE PRAISES, OR CENSURES
OF THIS WORLD.
STRANGER AS YOU RESPECT THE RECEPTACLE FOR THE DEAD.
(AS ONE OF THE MANY THAT WILL REST HERE,)
READ THE NAME OF
JOHN SAINT JOHN LONG
WITHOUT COMMENT.

Lionel Lockyer, died 1672, aged 72

Here LOCKYER *lies interr'd, enough his name*
Speaks, one hath few competitors in fame;
A name so great, so general it may scorn
Inscriptions which do vulgar tombs adorn!
A diminution 'tis to write in verse
His eulogies which most men's mouths rehearse;
His virtues and his pills are so well known,
That envy can't confine them under stone;
But they'll survive his dust, and not expire
Till all things else at the universal fire.
This verse is lost, his pills embalm him safe,
To future times without an epitaph.

Southwark Cathedral, London

Simon Furrier,
died 1750, aged 51

A Span is all that we can boast,
An Inch or two of Time;
Man is but Vanity and Dust,
In all his Flow'r and Prime.

Shoreditch, London

Above Kensal Green Cemetery, London
Below The graves of the Medhurst family, Lewes, Sussex

Alderman William Levins, died 1616

What others singly wish, Age, Wisdom, Wealth,
  Children to propagate their Names and Blood,
Chief Place in City oft, unphysick'd Health,
  And that which seasons all, the Name of Good;
In LEVINS *were all mixt, yet all are gone,*
Only the good Name lasts: That look upon.

All Hallows, London Wall, London

Edward Trelawney, barrister, died 1639

Oh! what a bubble, vapour, puff of breath,
A nest of worms, a lump of pallid earth,
Is mud-walled man! Before we mount on high
We cope with change, we wander after day.
Here lyes an honest lawyer, wot you what
A thing for all the world to wonder at!

    This turf has drank a
        Widow's tear;
    Three of her husbands
        Slumber here.

Pelynt, Cornwall

Sir Rogers Manners, died 1632

A living academie was this Knight
Divinitye, the arts, the toungs, what might
In learned schooles exactly, be profest
Tooke up their lodginge in his Noble breast
Till death like Church distroyers did pull downe
MANNERS, *true fabricque and the arts renowne.*

Whitwell, Derbyshire

Sir Allen Cotton,
Lord Mayor of London, died 1628

When he left earth, rich bounty dy'd,
Mild courtesie gave place to pride;
Soft mercie to bright justice sayde,
O sister! we are both betray'd:
White innocence lay on the ground,
By truth, and wept at either's wound;
The sons of Levi did lament,
Their lamps went out, their oil was spent;
Heav'n hath his soul, and only we
Spin out our lives in misery;
So death, thou missest of thy ends,
And kill'st not him, but kill'st his friends.

Chipping Ongar, Essex

Martha Tyrrell, died 1690

Could this stone speake it would the reader tell
She that lyes here did her whole sex excell ;
And why should death, with a promiscuous hand,
At one rude stroake impoverish a land ?

East Horndon, Essex

Margaret Robinson,
died 1816, aged 38

This Maid no Elegance of
*   Form possessed ;*
No earthly Love defiled her
*   sacred Breast.*
Hence free she lived from
*   the Deceiver Man :*
Heaven meant it as a Blessing.
*   She was plain.*

Warrington, Cheshire

Here lieth the bodies of THOMAS CAREW Esquire
and ANNE his wife who deceased the 6th and
8th day of December anno domini 1656.

Two bodies lie beneath this stone
Whom love and marriage long made one
One soul conjoined them by a force
Above the power of death's divorce,
One flame of love their lives did burn
Even to ashes in their urn.
They die but not depart who meet
In wedding and in winding sheet:
Whom God hath knit so firm in one
Admit no separation.
Therefore unto one marble trust
We leave their now united dust
As roots on earth embrace to rise
Most lovely flowers in Paradise.

Haccombe, Devon

John, James and Ann Howse, died 1691

Within this Little Howse three howses lye
John Howse, James Howse, ye short-liv'd twins, & I
Anne, of John Howse once ye endeared wife
Who lost mine owne To give those Babes their Life.
We three though Dead yet speake & put in mind
The Husband Father, whome we left behind
That we were howses only made of clay,
And calld For, could no longer Here stay,
But were layd Here to take our rest & ease
By Death, who taketh whome & where he please.

Langford, Oxfordshire

Philip Kinge, died 1592

The aged root that twelve times fruit did beare,
  (Though first and last were blasted in their prime)
Is wither'd now, and warnes his children deare,
  Though yet they spring, to know their winter's time.

  So labour'd he, and so is gone to rest;
  So liv'd, so dyed, as all (but cursed) blest.
Blesse, Lord! his fellow roote, that lives as yet,
  But as a vine without her prop decayes:
And blesse their branches, which these two did gett,
  And send them sapp to nourish them allwayes:
  Blesse roote and branch, that all may grow in thee,
  And meet at length to eat of thy life tree.

Worminghall, Oxfordshire

Here lyeth the body of
John Ap Robert, Ap Porth, Ap
David, Ap Griffith, Ap David
Vaughan, Ap Blethyn, Ap
Griffith, Ap Meredith,
Ap Jerworth, Ap Llewellyn,
Ap Jerom, Ap Heilin, Ap
Cowryd, Ap Cadvan, Ap
Alawgwa, Ap Cadell, The
King of Powys, Who
Departed This Life, The
xx Day of March, In The
Year Of Our Lord God
1642, And Of
His Age xcv.

Llanrhaeadr, Clwyd

John Milne, died 1667, aged 56

GREAT *artisan, grave senator,* JOHN MILNE
Renown'd for learning, prudence, parts, and skill;
Who in his life VITRUVIUS' *art had shown,*
Adorning other monuments; his own
Can have no other beauty than his name,
His memory, and everlasting fame.
Rare man he was, who could unite in one,
Highest and lowest occupation;
To sit with statesmen, counsellor to kings,
To work with tradesmen in mechanic things,
Majestic man, for person, wit, and grace,
This generation cannot fill his place.
Reader, JOHN MILNE, *who maketh the fourth* JOHN,
And by descent from father unto son,
Sixth master-mason to a royal race
Of seven successive kings, sleeps in this place.

Grey Friars, Edinburgh

Here lyes the bodeys of George Young
and Isabel Guthrie, and all their posterity
for fifty years backwards. November 1757.

Montrose, Angus

Sir Philip Sidney, killed in battle 1586, aged 32

England, Netherland, the Heavens, and the Arts,
The Souldiers and the World have made sixe parts
Of noble Sidney; for who will suppose,
That a small heape of stones can Sidney inclose!

England hath his body, for she it fed;
Netherland his bloud, in her defence shed:
The Heavens have his soule, the Arts have his fame,
The Souldiers the griefe, the Worlde his good name.

Old St Paul's, London

FULKE GREVILLE, died 1628, aged 74

Here lies the Body of
Fulke Greville,
Servant to Queen Elizabeth, Counsellor to King James
and Friend to Sir Philip Sydney.

St Mary's, Warwick, Warwickshire

Without a Name, for ever senseless, dumb,
Dust, Ashes, nought else lies within this Tomb:
Where-e'er I liv'd, or dy'd, it matters not,
To whom related, or of whom begot.
I was, but am not; ask no more of me;
'Tis all I am, and all that you must be.

Gravesend, Kent

Here lie the bodies
Of THOMAS BOND, and MARY his wife.
She was temperate, chaste, charitable,
BUT
She was proud, peevish, and passionate.
She was an affectionate wife, and a tender mother;
BUT
Her husband and child, whom she loved,
Seldom saw her countenance without a disgusting frown;
Whilst she received visitors, whom she despised,
With an endearing smile.
Her behaviour was discreet towards strangers,
BUT
Imprudent in her family.
Abroad, her conduct was influenced by good breeding
BUT
At home by ill temper.
She was a professed enemy to flattery,
And was seldom known to praise or commend;
BUT
The talents in which she principally excelled,
Were difference of opinion, and
Discovering flaws and imperfections.
She was an admirable economist,
And, without prodigality,
Dispensed plenty to every person in her family;
BUT
Would sacrifice their eyes to a farthing candle.
She sometimes made her husband happy
With her good qualities;
BUT
Much more frequently miserable,
With her many failings;
Insomuch, that in thirty years cohabitation,
He often lamented,
That maugre all her virtues
He had not, in the whole, enjoyed
Two years of matrimonial comfort.
AT LENGTH,
Finding she had lost the affections of her husband,
As well as the regard of her neighbours,
Family disputes having been divulged by servants,
She died of vexation, July 20, 1768, aged 48.
Her worn-out husband survived her
Four months and two days,
And departed this life, Nov. 28, 1768, aged 54.
WILLIAM BOND, brother to the deceased,
Erected this stone,
As a weekly monitor to the surviving
Wives of this parish,
That they may avoid the infamy
Of having their memories handed down to posterity,
With a patchwork character.

St John, Horsleydown,
Bermondsey, London

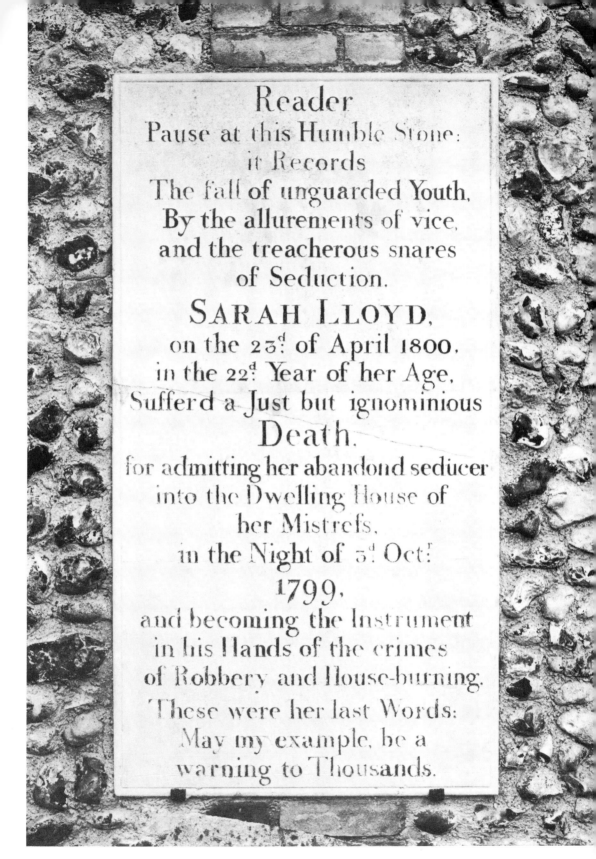

Reader
Pause at this Humble Stone:
it Records
The fall of unguarded Youth,
By the allurements of vice,
and the treacherous snares
of Seduction.
SARAH LLOYD,
on the 23.ᵈ of April 1800.
in the 22.ᵈ Year of her Age,
Suffer'd a Just but ignominious
Death.
for admitting her abandond seducer
into the Dwelling House of
her Mistrefs,
in the Night of 3.ᵈ Oct.ʳ
1799,
and becoming the Instrument
in his Hands of the crimes
of Robbery and House-burning,
These were her last Words:
May my example, be a
warning to Thousands.

Bury St Edmunds Cathedral, Suffolk

HERE LIETH THE
BODY OF Sᵗ EDMVND
FETIPLACE KNIGHT
SONNE AND HEYRE
TO WILLIAM FETI
PLACE ESQVIER
HE ESPOSED ANNE
DAVGHTER OF ROGER
ALFORDE ESQVIER

HE FIRD ISSVE IA
SONNES AND 7 DA
ERS HE APOINED TIS
TOMBE TO BE M
FOR HIM
ISE⁰ HIS
ORS HE E
HE 20 DA
IVNE A⁰

NVLL OVE
VME

HEARE LIETH THE BODY EOF WILLIAM   FETIPLACE E SQVIER SONNE AN⁰ HEYR
OF ALEXANDER FETIPLACE ESQVIER HE   POWSED ELIZABETH ASHFIELD DAVGHTER AN⁰
HEYR OF SEDMVN⁰ ASHFIELD KNIGHTE HAD   SVES SONNS HE DECEASE⁰ FEI DAY OF MAY 1508

HEARE LYETH THE BODY OF ALEXANDER   FETIPLACE SONNE AN⁰ HEYRE OF ANTHO
NYE FETIPLACE ESQVIER HE WAS FIRST ESPO   WSE⁰ IOANE DAVGHTER AN⁰ HEYR OF WILLIAM
ESQVIER FENTO⁰ORITY ASHIL⁰ HE HA⁰ ISVE 5S⁰ NNS AN⁰ DAVGHTERS HE DISCESE⁰ FEI 2 OF SEPTEMBER 1504

IN PIOVS MEMORIE
OF S^R EDMVND FETIPLACE ·KNIGHT·ON

READ:AND RECORD·RARE EDMVND FETIPLACE:
A KNIGHT RIGHT WORTHY OF HIS RANK & RACE:
WHOSE PRVDENT MANEGE IN TWO HAPPIE RAIGNES
WHOSE PVBLIQVE SERVICE & WHOSE PRIVATE PAINES:
WHOSE ZEALE, TO GOD·& TOWARDS ILL SEVERITIE
WHOSE TEMPERANCE WHOSE IVSTICE, WHOSE SINCERITIE:
WHOSE NATIVE MYLDNES, TOWARDS GREAT AND SMALL:
WHOSE FAITH & LOVE TO FRENDS, WIFE CHILDREN, ALL:
IN LIFE AND DEATH MADE HIM BELOVED, AND DEER
TO GOD AND MENN: AND EVER FAMOVS HEER:
BLESSED IN SOVLE IN BODIE GOODS, AND NAME
IN PLENTIEOVS PLANTS BY A MOST VERTVOVS DAME
WHO WITH HIS HEIRE AS TO HIS WORTH STILL DEBTER
BVILT HIM THIS TOOMB BVT IN HER HEART A BETTER

The Fettiplace monuments, Swinbrook, Oxfordshire

In the yeare 1653
When all thinges sacred were throughout ye nation
Either demolisht or profaned
Sr Robert Shirley Barronet
Founded this church;
Whose singular praise it is
to have done the best things in ye worst times
and
hoped them in the most callamitous
The righteous shall be had in everlasting remembrance

Sir Robert Shirley Bt,
who died in the Tower of London, 1656

In the yeare 1653
When all things sacred were throughout the nation
Either demollisht or profaned
Sir Robert Shirley Barronet
Founded this Church
Whose singular praise it is
to have done the best thinges in the worst times
And
hoped them in the most callamitous
The righteous shall be had in everlasting remembrance.

Staunton Harold, Leicestershire

Staunton Harold church with Shirley inscription

Here lies the body of Joan Carthew,
Born at St. Columb, died at St. Kew.
Children she had five,
Three are dead, and two alive,
Those that are dead chusing rather
To die with their Mother
Than live with their Father.

St Agnes, Cornwall

Here lies a modell of frail man,
A tender infant, but a span
In age or stature. Here she must
Lengthen out both bedded in dust.
Nine months imprisioned in the wombe
Eight on earth's surface free ; the tomb
must now complete her diarie,
So leave her to aeternitie.

Windsor, Berkshire

Marie Tucker, died in childbirth 1656,
by her husband.

My son and her t'enjoy together
Was too much bliss for me poor sinner,
And from her to have birth and breeding
For thee, son, both were too exceeding.
That some supplie we may God grant,
Make each to other of our want,
That I in thee my wife may see
That thou mayst find thy mother in me.

Doulting, Somerset

Nigh to the River Ouse, in York's fair City,
Unto this pretty Maid, Death shew'd no Pity;
As soon as she'd her Pail with Water fill'd,
Came sudden Death and Life like Water spill'd.

St Mary, Castlegate, York

Letitia Wayne, died 1771, aged 22

Underneath this Stone doth lie
As much Virtue as could die;
Approv'd by all, and lov'd so well,
Tho' Young, like Fruit that's ripe, she fell.

Hammersmith, London

Mrs Grace Toll, died 1757, aged 57

From earliest Youth in Virtue's path she trod,
Humbly conversed with and adored her God;
From Reason's shining light she never swerved,
Fair truth and goodness equally preserved.
To Wit that charm'd, a manly sense was join'd,
Ease graced her speech, and purity her mind.
Religious, Pious, Just, with every Art,
That mends the soul and opens wide the heart;
With Virtues that no malice could offend,
The safest guide and the sincerest friend,
With knowledge that could please and entertain,
All but the Dull and Spiteful, Proud and Vain,
Admired, Beloved, Lamented, here she Sleeps,
Who knew her – Loved her – and who Loved her Weeps.

Odiham, Hampshire

Mary and Tabitha Griffiths, died 1770

Their Flesh shall slumber in the Ground,
Till the last Trumpet's joyful Sound;
Then burst their Chains with sweet Surprize,
And in their Saviours Image rise.

Eltham, Kent

Mr and Mrs Snelling

IN *this cold bed, here consummated are*
The second nuptials, of a happy pair,
Whom envious Death once parted, but in vain,
For now himself has made them one again;
Here wedded in the grave, and, 'tis but just,
That they that were one flesh, should be one dust.

St Peter's, Canterbury, Kent

Here lieth the bodies of MRS. ANNA AND
MRS. DOROTHY FREEBORNE, wives of
Mr Samuel Freeborne, who departed
this life, one on the 31st of July 1641,
the other August the 20th 1658,
one aged 33 years, the other 44.

Under this stone two precious gems do lie,
Equal in weight, worth, lustre, and sanctity;
Yet perhaps one of them do excell;
Which was't who knows? ask him that knew them well.
By long enjoyment. If he thus be pressed
He'll pause, then answer; truly both were best;
Wer't in my choice that either of the twain
Might be returned to me to enjoy again,
Which should I choose? Well, since I know not whether,
I'll mourn for the loss of both, but wish for neither.
Yet here's my comfort, herein lies my hope,
The time a coming Cabinets shall ope.
Which are locked fast; then shall I see
My Jewels to my joy, my Jewels me.

Prittlewell, Essex

Know, Posterity, that on the 8th of April,
in the Year of Grace 1757, the rambling
Remains of JOHN DALE were,
in the 86th Year of his Pilgrimage,
laid upon his two Wives.

This Thing, in Life, will raise some Jealousy;
Here all Three lie together lovingly:
But from Embraces here no Pleasure flows,
Alike are here all human Joys and Woes.
Here Sarah's Chiding John no longer hears,
And old John's Rambling Sarah no more fears:
A Period comes to all their toilsome Lives;
The good Man's quiet; still are both his Wives.

Bakewell, Derbyshire

George Boulter, died *c.* 1780, aged 81

Underneath the corruptible parts of
a Vicar, one Husband, two Helpmeets,
both Wives and both Anns,
a Triplicity of Persons in two Twains,
but one Flesh,
are interred.

Kempsey, Hereford and Worcester

Robert Brigham, died 1685, aged 54

In youth I poor and much neglected went,
My grey and wealthy age in mirth I spent;
To honours then I courted was by many,
Although I did in no wise seek for any.
But what is now that wealth, that mirth, that glow,
Alas 'tis grave, 'tis dust, 'tis mourning now,
Unless my soul, through Christ, a place enjoys,
Where blessed saints with him in God rejoice.

Norwich, Norfolk

Robert Tewart, died 1694

The Poor, the World, Heav'n, and the Grave,
His Alms, his Praise, his Soul and Body have.

Easington, Humberside

John Geddes, died 1689

Grace me good : in hope I bide.

This world is a city
    full of streets, and
Death the merchant
    that all men meets.
If life were a thing
    that money could buy,
The poor could not live
    and the rich
    would not die.

Elgin Cathedral, Moray

Elizabeth Ireland, died 1779

Here I lie, at the chancel door,
Here I lie because I'm poor.
The farther in, the more you pay ;
Here lie I as warm as they.

Ashburton, Devon

Sir Cope D'Oyly, died 1633

To the glorious Memorie of that Noble Knight
Sir COPE D'OYLY, late Deputy Lieut. of
Oxfordshire & Justice of Oyer & Terminer,
Heir of the Antient & famous Family of
the D'Oyly's of the same Countie, Founders
of the Noble Abbies of Osney & Missenden, &c.

ASK *not of me, who's buried here?*
Goe ask the commons, ask the shiere,
Goe ask the church, they'll tell thee who,
As well as blubber'd eyes can do.
Goe ask the heraulds of the poor,
Thine ears shall hear enough to ask no more.
Then if thine eyes bedew this sacred urne,
Each drop a pearl will turn,
T' adorn his tomb; or if thou cans't not vent,
Thou bring'st more marble to his monument.

WOULD'ST *thou, Reader, draw to life*
The perfect copy of a wife,
Read on; and then redeem from shame
That lost, but honourable name.
This was once in spirit a Jael,
Rebecca in grace, in heart an Abigail,
In works a Dorcas, to the church a Hannah,
And to her spouse Susanna;
Prudently simple, providently wary,
To the world a Martha, and to heaven a Mary.

Hambleden, Buckinghamshire

Effigy of Sir William Wilcote and
his wife, North Leigh, Oxfordshire

A

Say what a Wife should be
and She was that.

B

No Epitaph nede make the iuſt man famde
The good are praysed when theyr only namd

C

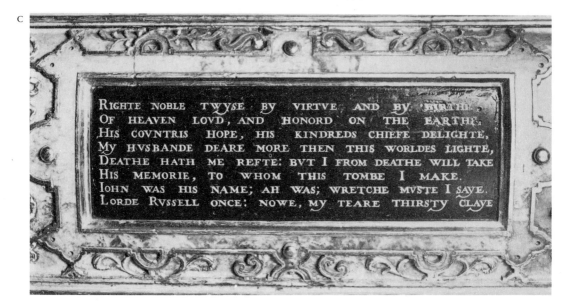

RIGHTE NOBLE TWYSE BY VIRTVE AND BY BIRTH,
OF HEAVEN LOVD, AND HONORD ON THE EARTHE,
HIS COVNTRIS HOPE, HIS KINDREDS CHIEFE DELIGHTE,
MY HVSBANDE DEARE MORE THEN THIS WORLDES LIGHTE,
DEATHE HATH ME REFTE: BVT I FROM DEATHE WILL TAKE
HIS MEMORIE, TO WHOM THIS TOMBE I MAKE.
IOHN WAS HIS NAME; AH WAS; WRETCHE MVSTE I SAYE.
LORDE RVSSELL ONCE: NOWE, MY TEARE THIRSTY CLAYE

D

MORIENTI CVNCTA QVIESCVNT
BEATI QVI MORIVNTVR IN DOMINO

BEHOWLDE YOVRE SELVES BY VS SVTCHE ONCE WERE WE AS YOV
AND YOV IN TYME SHALBE EVEN DVSTE AS WE ARE NOW

A St Mary's, Bury St Edmunds, Suffolk
C Monument to Lord John Russell
   Westminster Abbey

B Brass to Sir William Savile, Bakewell, Derbyshire
D Monument to Percival Smalpace,
   St Bartholomew the Great, City of London

Great Tew, Oxfordshire

Sir William Dyer, died 1641

My dearest dust, could not thy hasty day
Afford thy drowsy patience leave to stay
One hour longer, so that we might either
Have sat up or gone to bed together!
But since thy finished labour hath possessed
Thy weary limbs with early rest
Enjoy it sweetly; and thy widow bride
Shall soon repose her by thy slumbering side!
Whose business now is to prepare
My nightly dress and call to prayer.
Mine eyes wax heavy, and the days grow old,
The dew falls thick – my blood grows cold –
Draw, draw the closed curtains, and make room,
My dear, my dearest, dust, I come, I come.

Written by Lady Dyer
Colmworth, Bedfordshire

Tomb of Sir William and Lady Dyer

Mrs Aphra Behn, playwright,
died 1690, aged 49

Here lies a Proof that Wit can never be
Defence enough against Mortality.

Westminster Abbey, London

Elizabeth Emma Thomas, died 1808, aged 27

She had no fault save what travellers give the moon:
Her light was lovely, but she died too soon.

Islington, London

Martha Dias

Here lies the body of Martha Dias,
Who was always uneasy, and not over pious;
She liv'd to the age of threescore and ten,
And gave that to the worms she refus'd to the men.

Shrewsbury, Shropshire

Mrs Elizabeth Corbet, died 1724

Here rests a Woman good without Pretence,
Blest with plain Reason, and with sober Sense!
No Conquests she, but o'er herself desir'd,
No Arts essay'd, but not to be admir'd.
Passion and Pride were to her Soul unknown,
Convinc'd that Virtue only is our own.
So unaffected, so compos'd, a Mind;
So firm, yet soft; so strong, yet so refin'd;
Heaven as its purest Gold, by Tortures tried;
The Saint sustain'd it, but the woman died.

Written by Alexander Pope,
St Margaret's, Westminster, London

Mary Broomfield, died 1755, aged 80

The chief concern of her life for the last
twenty-five years was to order and provide
for her funeral. Her greatest pleasure
was to think and talk about it. She lived
many years on a pension of 9d per week,
and yet she saved £5, which at her own
request was laid out on her funeral.

Macclesfield, Cheshire

He after a long & painful illness is
now envellaped in sod and solitary
Stillness youth stay a wile and think
On time every moment shortens day
every pulse beats life away i began
in youth the world to rome and finished
in manhood at the tomb

Little Dean, Gloucestershire

Unknown, dated 1690

Thus youth, and age, and all things pass away,
Thy turn is now as his was yesterday :
Tomorrow shall another take thy room,
The next day he a prey for worms become :
And on your dusty bones shall others tread,
As now you walk and trample on the dead,
Till neither sign or memory appear,
That you had ever birth or being here.

North Mimms, Hertfordshire

William Burnet, died 1760, aged 75

To-day he's drest in Gold or Silver bright,
Wrapp'd in a Shrowd before To-morrow Night;
To-day he's feasting in delicious Food,
To-morrow Nothing eats can do him good;
To-day he's nice, and scorns to feed on Crumbs,
In a few Days himself's a Dish for Worms;
To-day he's honour'd and in great Esteem,
To-morrow not a Beggar values him;
To-day he rises from a Velvet Bed,
To-morrow he's in one that's made of Lead;
To-day his House, tho' large, he thinks too small,
To-morrow can command no House at all;
To-day has twenty Servants at his Gate,
To-morrow scarcely one will deign to wait;
To-day perfum'd, and sweet as is the Rose,
To-morrow stinks in ev'ry Body's Nose;
To-day he's grand, majestic, all Delight,
Ghastly and pale before To-morrow Night.
Now what you've wrote, and said whate'er you can,
This is the best that you can say of Man.

Croydon, Surrey

Captain Nicholas Tattersell,
Through whose prudence, valour, and loyalty
Charles the Second, King of England,
After he had escaped the sword of his merciless
rebels
And his forces received a fatal overthrow
At Worcester, Sep. 3, 1651
Was faithfully preserved, and conveyed to France;
Departed this life 26th July, 1674.

Within this marble monument doth lie
Approved faith, honour, and loyalty:
In this cold clay he has now taken up his station,
Who once preserved the church, the crown, and nation.
When Charles the great was nothing but a breath,
This valiant soul stept in twixt him and death:
Usurper's threats, nor tyrant's rebel frown,
Could not affright his duty to the crown;
Which glorious act of his for Church and State,
Eight princes in one day did gratulate;
Professing all to him in debt to be,
As all the world are to his memory.
Since earth could not reward the worth him given,
He now receives it from the King of Heaven.
In the same chest one jewel more you have,
The partner of his virtue, bed, and grave.

Brighton, Sussex

James Agee and John Park,
executed 1685

Stay, passenger, as thou goest by,
And take a look where these do lie ;
Who for the love they bare to truth,
Were depriv'd of their life and youth.
Tho' laws made then caus'd many die,
Judges, and 'sizars were not free,
He that to them did these delate,
The greater count he hath to make :
Yet no excuse to them can be ;
At ten condemn'd, at two to die.
So cruel did their rage become,
To stop their speech caus'd beat the drum.
This may a standing witness be,
'Twixt presbyt'ry and prelacy.

Paisley, Renfrewshire

John James, died 1707

Here lyeth John James the old Cook of Newby,
who was a faithful Servant to his Master,
and an upright, downright honest Man.

Banes among Stanes,
do lie sou still,
Whilk the Soul wanders
E'en where God will.

Ripon Cathedral, North Yorkshire

Thomas Cotes, died 1648

Honest old Thomas Cotes, that sometime was
Porter at Ascott hall, hath now (alas)
Left his key, lodg, fyre, friends, & all, to have
A roome in Heaven. This is that good man's grave.
Reader, prepare for thine, for none can tell
But that you two may meete to night. Farewell.

He dyed the 20th of │ Set up at the apoyntment
November 1648 │ and charges of his friend
Geo: Houghton.

Wing, Buckinghamshire

Samuel Bridger, died 1650

Receiver of this College Rents, he paid
His Debt to Nature, and beneath he's laid
To rest, until his summons to remove,
At the last Audit, to the Choir above.

Gloucester Cathedral, Gloucestershire

John Broadbent, sexton, died 1769, aged 73

Forty-eight years, strange to tell,
He bore the bier and toll'd the bell,
And faithfully discharged his trust,
In "earth to earth" and "dust to dust."
    Cease to lament,
    His life is spent,
The grave is still his element;
His old friend Death knew 'twas his sphere,
So kindly laid the sexton here.

Saddleworth, West Yorkshire

Francis Thwaites,
died 1700, aged 2

As carefull nurses
To their bed doe lay
Their children which too
Long would wanton play :
Soe to prevent all my
Evening crimes,
Nature my Nurse laid
Me to bed betimes.

Stanford,
Nottinghamshire

Detail from the Manners tomb, Bakewell, Derbyshire

IN MEMORY, OF Mʳ THŌ: SMITH, OF ELMLY-LOVET, IN Yᵉ COVNTY OF WOR= CESTER, & BACH: OF ARTS, LATE OF CH: CH: OXFORD. WHO THROVGH Yᵉ SPOTTED VAILE OF ĦE SMALL-POX, RENDRED A PVRE, & VN= SPOTTED SOVL TO GOD. EXPECTING, BVT NOT FEARING DEATH; Wᶜᴴ ENDED HIS DAYEˢ, MARCH ĦE 10ᵀᴴ ANNO DŌM 1663¾ ÆTATIS SVÆ 27.

The Virtues which in his short life were shown, haue equalld been by few, surpasſd by none

Above Westminster Abbey

Opposite, above Yarnton, Oxfordshire

Below Tewkesbury Abbey, Gloucestershire

Opposite, below Newnham-upon-Severn, Gloucestershire

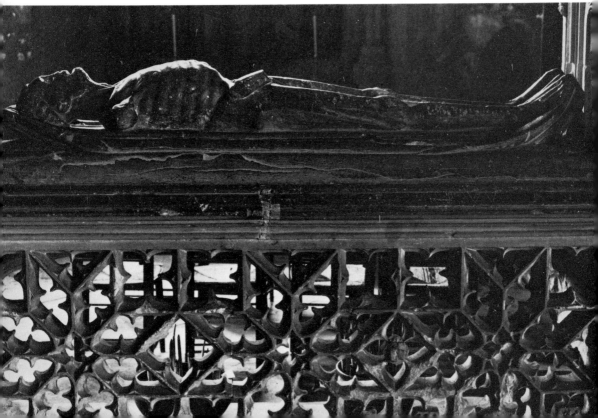

No friendship dieth
With death of any day,
No true friendship lieth
Cold unto lifeless clay.

Though on a boyhood's playtime
Be gone with summer's breath,
No friendship fades with Maytime,
No friendship dies with death.

SWEET THOU ART SLEEPING
CRADLED ON MY HEART.
SAFE IN GOD'S KEEPING
WHILE I MUST WEEP APART.

THORNTON

In memory
of
John King
who departed this Life 29th of
December 1774 aged 75 years.
He was 61 years Servant
to
Mr. Francis Valentine,
Joseph
Valentine, and Paul
Valentine,
from Father to Son,
without ever
Quitting their Service,
Neglecting
his Duty, or being
Disguised
in Liquor.

Beckenham, Kent

To the Memory of
David Wall,
whose superior performance on the
bassoon endeared him to an
extensive musical acquaintance.
His social life closed on the
4th Dec., 1796, in his 57th year.

Ashover, Derbyshire

Above G. F. Watts Memorial Chapel, Compton, Surrey
Below Highgate Cemetery, London

Edward Lambe, died 1617

Edward	Edward Lambe	Lambe
Ever	Second son of	Lived
Envied	Thomas Lambe	Laudably
Evil	of Trimley	Lord
Endured	Esquire	Let
Extremities	all his days	Like
Even	he lived a Bachelor	Life
Earnestly	well learned in Divine	Learn
Expecting	and Common Laws	Ledede
Eternal	with his counsel he	Livers
Ease	helped many, yet took	Lament
	fees scarce of any	

East Bergholt, Suffolk

Ellen Reson, died 1630

The Charnel mounted on this W ⎫
Sits to be seen in Funer   ⎮
A Matron plain, Domestic   ⎮
In housewivery a princip   ⎮
In care and pains Continu   ⎮
Not slow, not gay, nor prodig ⎬ *ALL*
Yet neighbourly and hospit   ⎮
Her children seven, yet living ⎮
Her sixty-seventh year hence did c ⎮
To rest her body natur   ⎮
In hope to rise spiritu   ⎭

Hadleigh, Suffolk

Florens Caldwell, died 1590

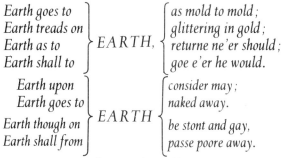

Earth goes to   ⎫   ⎧ as mold to mold;
Earth treads on ⎮   ⎮ glittering in gold;
Earth as to   ⎬ *EARTH*,   ⎨ returne ne'er should;
Earth shall to   ⎭   ⎩ goe e'er he would.

Earth upon   ⎫   ⎧ consider may;
Earth goes to   ⎮   ⎮ naked away.
Earth though on ⎬ *EARTH*   ⎨ be stont and gay,
Earth shall from ⎭   ⎩ passe poore away.

Be mercifull and charitable
Relieve the poor as thou art able
A shrowd to the grave
Is all thou shalt have.

St Martin's, Ludgate, London

Here lyeth the Body of Edward Sherland, of Gray's Inn,
Esqre, descended from the antient family of Sherland in the
Isle of Sheppey, in Kent; who lived the whole of his life a
single man, and dyed in this parish the 13th of May, 1609.

Tombes have no use, unlesse it be to showe
The due respect which friend to friend doth owe.
Tis not a mausolean monument
Or hireling epitaph that doth prevent
The flux of fame: a painted sepulcher
Is but a rotten trustlesse treasure,
A fair gate to oblivion.
But he whose life, whose everie action,
Like well-wrought stones and pyramides, erecte
A monument to honour and respecte,
As this man did; he needs none other herse,
Yet hath but due, having both tombe and verse.

Elmset, Suffolk

Near this Stone
are interred the remains of
Mr. DAVID HERD, Writer;

A Man of Probity,
Of a kind and friendly disposition,
Mild Tolerant principles,
And a taste in ancient Scottish Literature.
Not solicitous to shine,
Nor anxious to become rich,
He lost few friends,
And made few enemies.
These qualities had their influence;
For they averted many of the wants and evils
of declining years.

He died a Bachelor, aged 86
Upon the 10th of June 1810.

Old Calton Burial Ground, Edinburgh

To the memory of Ric: Richards who by Gangrene
lost first a Toe, afterwards a Leg, & lastly his Life
on the 7th day of Aprill, 1656.

Ah! cruell Death, to make three meales of one,
To taste and taste till all was gone.
But know, thou Tyrant, when the trumpe shall call,
He'll find his feet, & stand when thou shalt fall.

Banbury, Oxfordshire

Under this stone lieth the Broken
Remains of STEPHEN JONES who had
his leg cut off without the Consent of
Wife or Friends on the 23rd October,
1842, in which day he died. Aged 31 years.
Reader I bid you farewell. May
the Lord have mercy on you in the
day of trouble.

St John's, Chester, Cheshire

James Cobb, died 1769, aged 54

Cut off, my Friend, alas! tho' ripe in Years,
We mourn thy Fate, lament thee with our Tears;
In sympathetic Language talk thee o'er,
Thy Friendship and thy Worth we oft explore.
But what does That avail! 'Tis not our Grief
Can bring thee back, or give thee least Relief.
Take him for all in all, you'll rarely find
A better Heart, or a more gen'rous Mind.
Peace to his Soul! in Heaven let it rest,
And lay the Earth but lightly on his Breast!
In Tribute to thy Memory, receive
A Sigh, a Tear; 'tis all a Friend can give.

Bunhill Fields, London

Upon the death of the excellent and
pious Lady Lettice Countesse of Leicester
who dyed upon Christmas Day
in the morning 1634.

Looke in this vault and search it well
Much treasure in it lately fell
W.ee all are robd and all doe say
Our wealth was carried this away
And that the theft might nere be found
Tis buried closely under ground
Yet if you gently stirr the mould
There all our losse you may behould
There may you see that face that hand
Which once was fairest in the land
She that in her younger yeares
Matcht with two great English peares
She that did supply the warrs
With thunder and the court with stars
She that in her youth had bene
Darling to the Maiden Queene
Till she was content to quitt
Her favoure for her Favoritt
Whose gould threed when she saw spunn
And the death of her brave sonn
Thought it safest to retyre
From all care and vaine desire
To a private countrie cell
Where she spent her dayes soe well
That to her the better sort
Came as to an holy court
And the poore that lived neare
Dearth nor Famine could not feare
Whilst she liv'd she lived thus
Till that God displeas'd with us
Suffred her at last to fall
Not from Him but from us all
And because she tooke delight
Christs poore members to invite
He fully now requites her love
And sends His Angels from above
That did to Heaven her Soule convay
To solemnize His owne birth day.

St Mary's, Warwick, Warwickshire

William Collins, poet, died 1759, aged 39

Ye who the merits of the dead revere,
Who hold misfortune sacred, genius dear,
Regard this tomb, where Collins, hapless name!
Solicits kindness with a double claim.
Though nature gave him, and though science taught,
The fire of fancy, and the reach of thought;
Severely doom'd to penury's extreme,
He pass'd in maddening pains life's feverish dream;
While rays of genius only served to show
The thickening horror, and exalt his woe.
Ye walls that echoed to his frantic moan,
Guard the due record of this grateful stone.
Strangers to him, enamour'd of his lays,
This fond memorial to his talents raise;
For this the ashes of a bard require
Who touch'd the tenderest notes of pity's lyre,
Who join'd pure faith to strong poetic powers,
Who in reviving reason's lucid hours
Sought on one book his troubled mind to rest,
And rightly deem'd the book of God the best.

Chichester Cathedral, Sussex

Sir Edward and Lady Rodney, died 1657

Reader, behold this one made twaine,
By marriage once, by death againe –
Such noble, wise, and fortunate –
Inferior only unto fate :
And could this urn its silence breake,
Their tongues would mend what ours can speake –
This was that large and letter'd mind,
Where wise and just were so combin'd,
That his devoted country tooke
Him for their judge, councell, and booke ;
And while he liv'd, justice (tis known)
Resign'd her scales to him alone :
Blamelesse even in his enemies eyes,
Unless they griev'd he was too wise.
His ladie, to the virtuous dear,
Was only meete to be his peere ;
For moral parts and parentage
The most accomplish'd of her age –
Heav'n therefore destin'd them to have
One heart and bed, and now one grave.

Rodney Stoke, Somerset

The Killigrew Monument, Westminster Abbey

ROBERT KILLIGREW P . M .
in the County of Cornwall Esquire,
Son of THOMAS and CHARLOTTE.
Page of Honour to King Charles
the Second, Brigadier General of
her Majesty's Forces, Killed in
Spain in the Battle of Almanza
the 14.ᵗʰ day of April Anᵒ Dni.
1707. Ætatis Suæ 47.
Militavit annis 24.

Supremum   *munus frater*   *mœrens posuit*

IANE LISTER
dear childe
died Oct:-7th-1688

Above Westminster Abbey
Opposite Ely Cathedral, Cambridgeshire
Below Ruardean, Gloucestershire

Received of PHILIP HARDING
his borrowed earth
July 4th 1673.

Crudwell, Wiltshire

William Marchant,
died 1831, aged 50

I asked for life but was denied ;
I took it patiently and died.

Buckland Dinham,
Somerset

Here lieth Richard Dent
in his last tenement.

Finedon,
Northamptonshire

Burford, Oxfordshire

Hugo Fortescue, died 1625

Stay, Reader, stay, this structure seems t'invite
Thy wandering Eyes, on it to fixe thy sighte.
In this Pile's summit thou majst descrie
Heaven's all beholding & all guiding Eye
That sheds his benediction's gracious beames
Of Love & Goodness on these fruitfull streames
Of numerous issue, sprong from nuptiall tyes
With various antient worthy families.
Here is in briefe presented to thy viewe
The long liv'd race of honoured FORTESCUE
Combin'd in holyest rites, on Time's faire scroll
With CHICHESTER, *then* SPECCOTT, *last with*
   ROLLE.
And long & wide may sacred Grace and Fame
Produce & propagate this generous Name
That it may brooke what Honour gave in fielde
LE FORT ESCUE, *the strong & lasting Shielde.*
A Shielde not only their own righte to fence
But also to repell wrong's violence.
Which, that it may accordingly be done
Pray, Reader, pray GOD *be their Shielde & Sunne.*

Weare Giffard, Devon

Robert Longe, died 1620

The life of Mann is a trewe Lottarie,
Where venterouse Death draws forth lotts shorte & longe:
Yet free from fraude & partiall flatterie,
He shufl'd Sheildes of severall size amonge,
   Drewe LONGE : *& soe drewe longer his short daies,*
   Th' Auncient of daies beyonde all time to praise.

Broughton Gifford, Wiltshire

Sarah Dutry, died 1755

Such peerless Bloom, such Virtue without Flaw,
As Limners aim at when they Angels draw,
Such Nature did on her fair Frame dispense;
Excell'd by nought but her own Innocence:
Which from within beam'd so much native Grace,
The guileless Soul outshone the faultless Face.
 So when choice Diamonds, set in purest Gold,
 Their radiant Lustre to our Sight unfold,
 Th' enchanted Eye o'erlooks the costly Mould.
No Wonder, then, that such intrinsic Worth
Should be thus early ravish'd from the Earth.
Heav'n, jealous to preserve her spotless Mind
Unblemish'd still, left the rich Ore behind,
To mingle here with its parental Clay,
Till both resum'd shall blaze in endless Day;
And took mean Time her Soul, the precious Gem,
To fix it in his New Jerusalem.

Old St Pancras, London

ANNA HARRISON, died 1745, aged 80

ANNA HARRISON
Well known by the name of NAIMA RANN DANN,
Who was chaste, but no prude
And tho' free, yet no harlot,
By principle virtuous,
By education a protestant.
Her freedom made her liable to censure,
Whilst her extensive charities made her esteemed.
Her tongue and her hands were not governable,
But the rest of her members she kept in subjection.
After a life of 80 years thus spent,
She died Nov. 15th, 1745.
Passenger, weigh her virtues,
Be charitable,
And speak well of her.

Easingwold, North Yorkshire

Elizabeth Smith, died 1750, aged 15

Not far remote lies a lamented Fair,
Whom Heav'n had fashion'd with peculiar Care:
For Sense distinguish'd, and esteem'd for Truth,
And ev'ry winning Ornament of Youth.
Yet liv'd she free from Envy, and admir'd,
But ah! too soon she from the World retir'd.
Filial Affection rose in her so high,
No Sage can censure the parental Sigh.
The gen'rous Plant had shone in Beauty's Pride;
Gaily it bloom'd, but in the Blooming dy'd:
Learn from this Marble what thou valu'st most,
And set'st thy Heart upon, may soon be lost.

St Botolph, Aldersgate, London

Mary Wanley, died 1709, aged 60

Beneath this marble stone interr'd doth lie,
One of known diffusive charity:
She unto all was generous and free,
But to those that were poor especially;
None at the door would she let craving stay,
Or ever go without an alms away;
Nor did she only good in public view,
But frequently unask'd in private too.
What her right hand did freely thus bestow
So secret was, her left hand did not know,
She liberal was according to her store,
And ofttimes, griev'd because she gave no more.
In this alone, reader, I wish that you
Not only praise, but imitate her too.

Barningham, Norfolk

Lucie Bromfield, died 1618

The Husband speaking truly of his Wife,
Reads his Loss in her Death, her Praise in Life.

Here Lucie Quinbie Bromfield burried lies
With neighbours sad, weeping hearts, sighs, eyes
Children eleven, ten living, me she brought.
More kind, true chaste was none in deed and thought.
House, children, state by her was rul'd, bred thrives,
One of the best of Maids, women, wives.
Now gone to God, her heart sent long before
In Fasting, Pray'r, faith, hope and alms deeds store.
If any fault she loved me too much,
Ah pardon that, for there are too few such.
Then, Reader, if though not hard hearted be,
Praise God for her, but sigh and pray for me.
Here by her dead, I dead desire to lie,
Till rais'd to life we meet no more to die.

Titchfield, Hampshire

John Baret, died 1463

JOHN (*He that will sadly behold me with hys ie*) BARET
        (*Maye see his owne merowr and lerne to die.*)

Wrapped in a schete as a ful rewlie bretche,
No mor of al my mynde to meward wil stretche.
From erthe I kam, and on to erthe I am brought,
This is my natur: for of erthe I was wrought.
Thus erthe on to erthe tendeth to knet.
So endyth eche creture: quoth John Baret.

Wherfor ye pepil in waye of cherite
Wyth your gode praiers I praye ye helpe me.
For such as I am: right soe shalle ye al bi.
Now God on my sowle haue merci and pite. amen.

St Mary's, Bury St Edmunds, Suffolk

Christopher Henley, died 1693

Conceal'd from Care, beneath this Marble lies
His sacred Relicks, which again must rise;
Remote from human Discords unoppress'd,
In their cold Urn his peaceful Ashes rest:
Snatcht into Earth's dark Bosom, free from all
Those Troubles which a mortal Life befal.
O pious Reader! know his living just
Procures his quiet Slumbers in the Dust.
His virtuous Deeds crown his unthinking Clay,
Erect a Monument without Delay:
Raising his Soul to everlasting Day.

His Wife and Children's Grief their Tears reveal,
Each find their Loss too weighty to conceal.
No unjust Act thro' his whole Race we find,
Loving he liv'd, and just to all Mankind:
Easie he sleeps till Heaven shall raise his Dust,
Yielding his Soul to th' Mansions of the Just.

Stepney, London

Benjamin and Betty Coutes,
died 1796

Great God! is this our certain doom
And are we still secure?
Still walking downward to our tomb,
And yet prepare no more.

Wool, Dorset

George Henry, died 1771

A quiet Conscience in a quiet Breast,
Has only Peace, and only Peace of Rest;
Then close thine Eyes in Peace, and rest secure;
No Sleep so sweet as thine, no Rest so sure.

Acton, London

Dust from dust at first was taken, –
Dust by dust is now forsaken;
Dust in dust shall still remain,
Till dust from dust shall rise again.

Caernarvon, Gwynedd

Thomas Crabtree, died 1680, aged 19

Short was my Stay in this vain World,
All but a seeming Laughter ;
Therefore mark well thy Words and Ways,
For thou com'st posting after.

St Peter's, Leeds, West Yorkshire

What I spent, I had:
What I gave, I have:
What I kept, I lost.